Works of the Heart

A Collaboration From Many Creative People

First printing

At the specific preference of the authors, Lulu.com allowed this work to remain exactly as the authors intended, verbatim, without editorial input.
Any characters in this book are fictional, and are not based on any actual person.

Works of the Heart

ISBN:
978-1-105-38335-9

Copyright 2012

Riverview United Methodist Church
Elevator Project

Printed in the United States of America

All works in this book have been donated
to the Riverview United Methodist Church.

All proceeds from the sale of this book will go directly to
the RUMC Elevator Fund, and upon completion
of the Elevator Project will go to the
RUMC Apple Dumpling Fund.

Works of
the Heart

A Collaboration From Many Creative People

Priceless
Your voice is so pure and sweet
its like I am eating honey out of the jar.
Your eyes are so clear blue I swear
I am swimming when I look into them.
And I can't wait until I can hug you
cause I'm not going to want to let go.
You Are Priceless.
~Glenn Huff

I'M JUST A GIRL

It took me by surprise
when I at first laid eyes
on a stranger that suddenly entered my life

He pleased my heart
He touched my soul
He marked my life

How could a stranger do such a thing?
When all along it was just a while when I met him?

True it was awkward
Yet, it felt like an award
And it was more awarding
Each day I get a glimpse of him

I stand near him
Can't take my eyes off of him
Dreams is what it takes for me to really feel him
And for him to feel me

His name is written
on every piece of paper I have hidden
I wrote poems, wrote stories, heard songs
That I especially dedicated to him for long

I ate less
And my baggy eyes showed I was sleepless
I did almost everything less
but still tried to make him impressed

I've been waiting
for that special moment when he would be saying
those words I long to hear
for that special moment when he would be doing
those silly things I thought I never did
for that special moment when he would be feeling
those emotions I had for him

Am I exaggerating?
Am I acting foolish?
Am I to be made fun of?

What can I do?

I'm just a girl

~Kelly

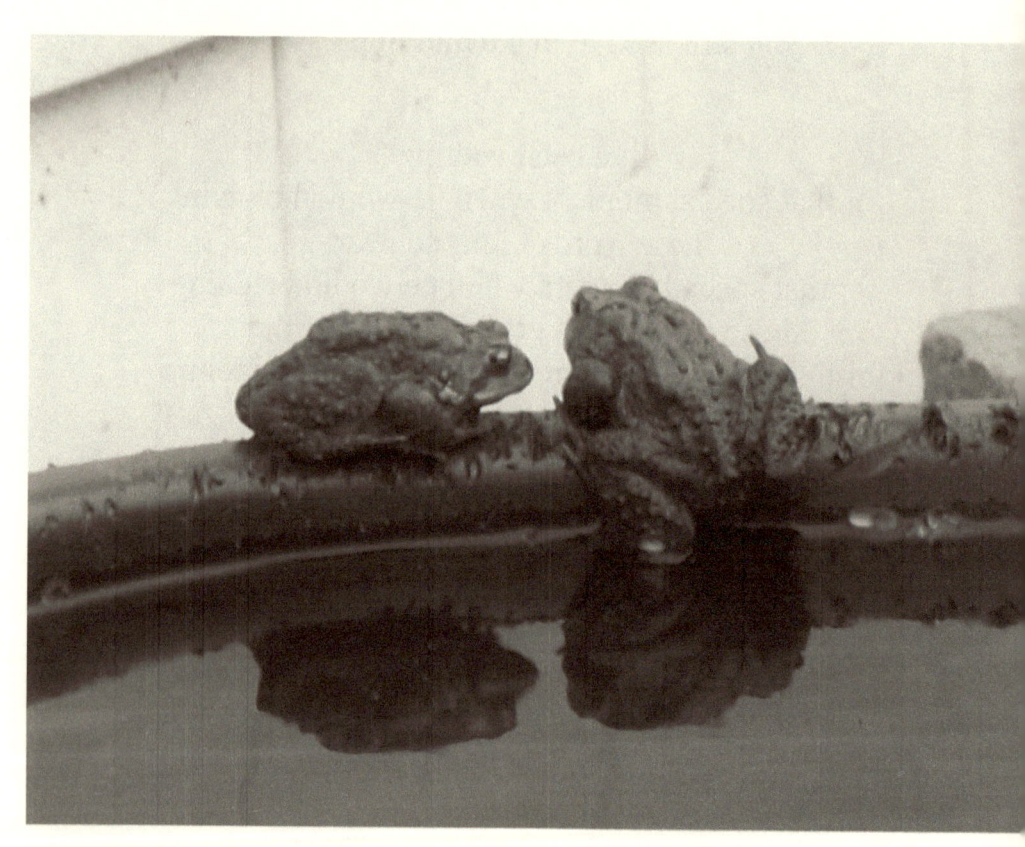

"Mom's Toads" by Angela Bradley

"Stand Up"

When doubts assail and troubles avail,
Stand firm, stand firm.
When priorities duel and perplexities rule,
Stand against, stand against.
When anxiety grows and fear overflows,
Stand tall, stand tall.
When evil abounds and darkness surrounds,
Stand back, stand back.
When ridiculed squarely and treated unfairly,
Stand still, stand still.
When temptation calls and worldliness appalls,
Stand upright, stand upright.
When peer pressures sway and friends fall away,
Stand out, stand out.
When death nears and eyes fill with tears,
Stand by, stand by.
When the wicked take the helm and events overwhelm,
Stand outside, stand outside.
So that when Jesus astounds and the trumpet resounds,
You will stand there, stand there.

— Jim Parkinson (1996)

Old Dodge City

The gallows looked so dark and gruesome
as he climbed the gallows stairs,
with the townsfolk all around it
sitting in their chairs.

As he reached the top of the stairs
he was not afraid of what lay ahead.
He knew that soon like others
he would be dead.

The hangman knew just what to do
as he reached the top,
he made him turn, and back up
then he made him stop.

The rope went around his neck with ease
as he gave the townsfolk glares.
As the reverend walked
towards the gallows stairs.

The hangman's hand was on the lever,
as he nodded he was ready.

Death came swift and quick
as he fell through the trap door.
He kicked and choked and then
he was no more.

They buried him the next day
in the cemetery on the hill.
The wind was cold and the birds were quiet
and everything was still.

Some thought his death to be justice.
Others thought it a pity.
But now he sleeps on Old Boothill
in the town of Dodge City.

-J.A. Sherbine

You always use to tease me,
And call me some mean names.
Then I got to know you,
But some things never change.

Everyone at school knows you,
That could be good or bad.
Depending on what happened,
You've made some people mad.

I got to know you better,
And heard about your pain.
Tonight I got a phone call,
Nothing will ever be the same.

I wish I knew what happened,
And why you did what you did.
"Oh Chris, if you could just tell me,
what was going on inside your head?"

"Nothing should ever seem so bad,
for a child to take their own life."
I quote that from a friend of mine,
Because I believe my friend is right.

Tomorrow as I walk through that school,
And see so many crying,
I'll hold back most of my tears,
Or at least I'll be trying.

Chris, please know we miss you,
And will for years to come.
Because it's irreversible,
We can't undo what you have done.

In Memory of
Christopher W. Hall
6/13/82-10/17/99

Chris is now in Heaven,
At least that's what I believe.
When he repents at Heaven's Gate,
God won't want him to leave.

~Angela Rae

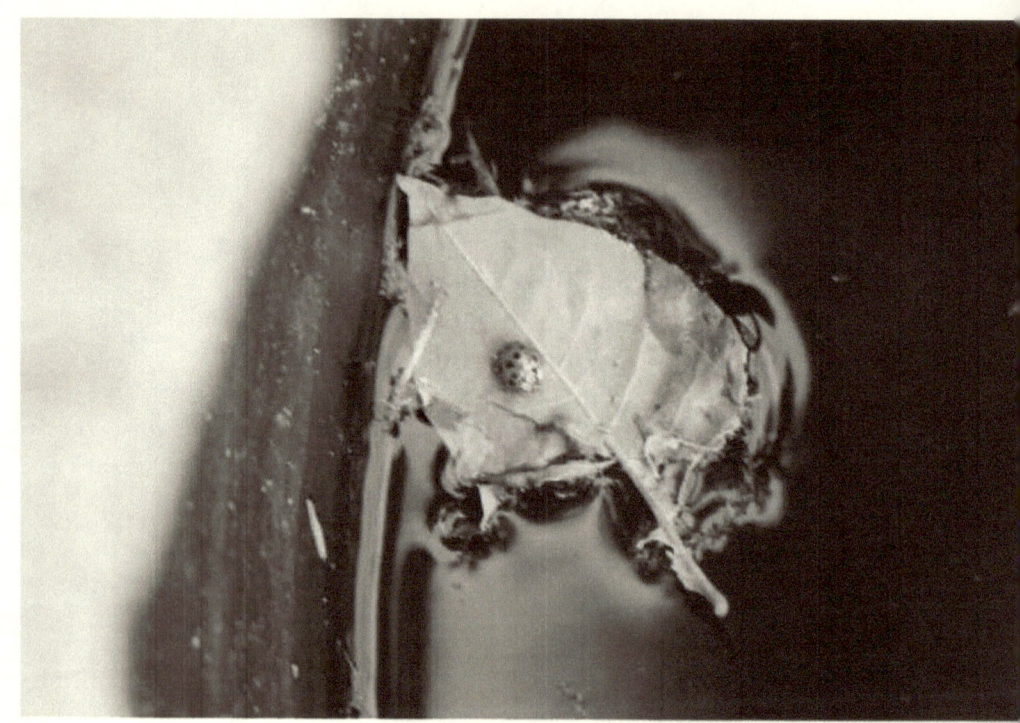

"Ladybug Journey" by Stephanie Gailey

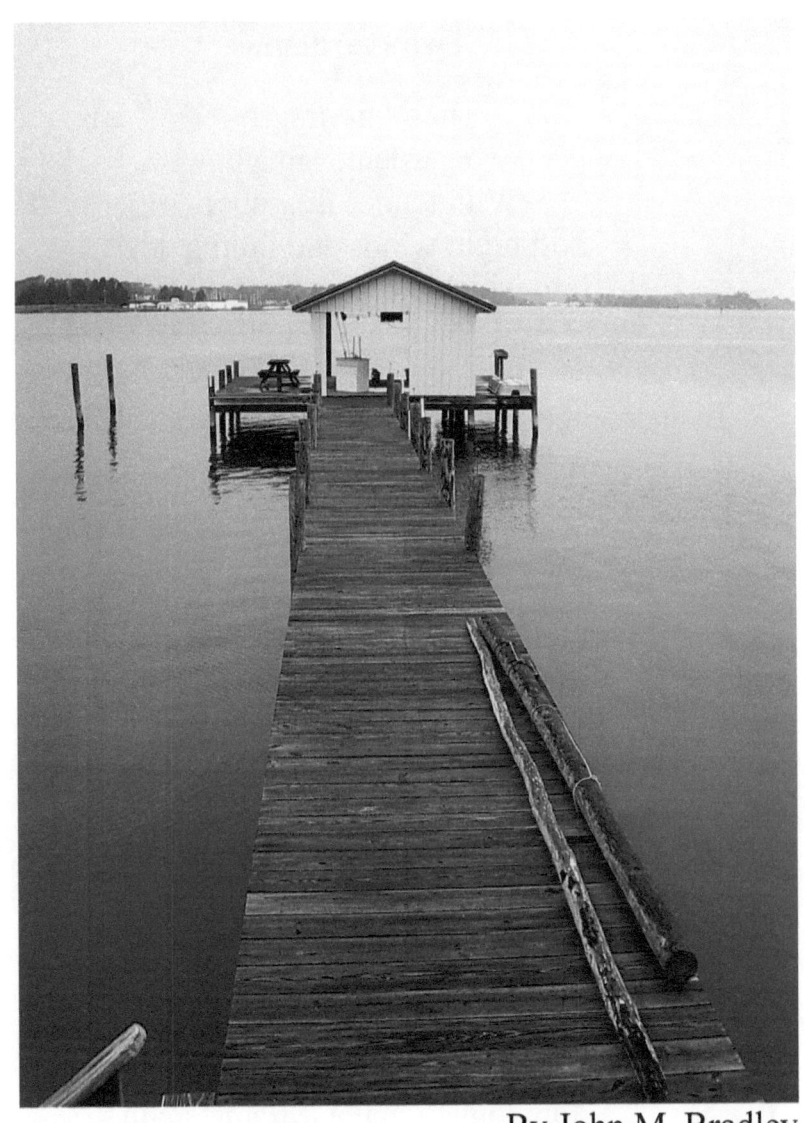

By John M. Bradley

Two Gardenias

These are fragile-
Two gardenias in a bowl
With tender fragrance.|
Soft night winds and falling dew
Into which old people cannot go,
And young are not allowed:
Soft haunting melodies,
Evanescent moons that one can almost see through.
Laughter ringing out.
Then all is still again,
And there is pain once more.
Determination and blind hopes
That tomorrow may be crushed and die,
As my two gardenias in a bowl
May wither and turn brown
Because someone dared to touch them.

These are secure-
Red roses that may be loved.
Pressed to my cheek they will not turn brown.
An open fireplace
That may burn low,
And yet there are always
More logs to make it flame again.
A cat asleep upon the hearth,
Contented, purring.
Sunshine, and flower gardens,
Laughter and voices singing,
Warm summer evenings.

All these, fragile and secure,
I love.

And if I choose security, then I must live without
Something to hope for,
For I shall have all I desire.
And there will be a longing,
And I shall want anxiety.

And if I choose fragility,
I shall know I have been foolish
Giving up the security I have
Always searched for.
And I shall crush my love,
And it may wither and die
Like my two gardenias
In a bowl,
Leaving me nothing but memories.
Security could always be there.
Yet fragility is as old as eternity,
And security has never been born.

And if I do not choose,
Then must I walk alone.

Then I must choose
And I shall choose my fragile things,
For I shall have memories that linger on
Like the fragrances of gardenias
When the flowers are faded and gone.
~ Alice Proudfit

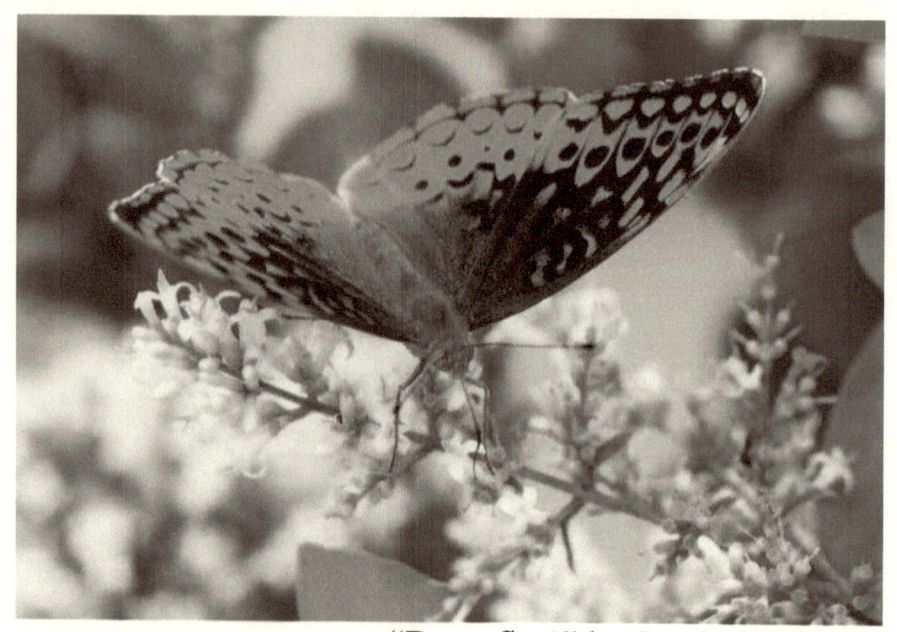

"Butterfly 1" by Stephanie Gailey

I'm sitting in a crack.
Can't go forward, can't jump back.

I wait for a sign
That one day you'll be mine.

I'm lonely and afraid.
It feels like I'm going insane!

I'm banging my head against a wall.
The whole sky, the whole world will fall!

I'd hope that my hand you would take.
But I'd fall alone, all for your love's sake.

On every candle and star I'll wish.
One day, It's me you'll want to kiss.

-Angela Robyn

What the Past Hides
The following is a short story by Jennifer Brown

The moment she set foot back on the familiar grounds of Lubique, Pennsylvania vivid images stole through her mind. Images she wished she could forget.

For the time being though, she needed to forget those memories. She was back here to do a job, then leave. It was as simple as that.

She stood outside the Macfield Hotel frozen, and staring up at the three story structure. It had been ten years since it happened. She had been 17, now she was 27.

She stayed in a room there with her best friend, Holly Kingford. Holly had won four tickets to a sold out show for Red Hot Chili Peppers, on the radio. Of course, she had been with Holly when she urged her to call and try to win them. Holly had said she'd never get through to win them. Three minutes later, they were both live on the air, and squealing with delight.

They had to find two other people to go with. Holly begged her to ask her brother to go. "This is supposed to be fun!" she argued with Holly. "Oh, but it *will* be fun," Holly had countered. "You can ask Warner to go."

"Trinity?"

The familiar voice startled her from her thoughts, and she whirled around, facing a much older looking, but still just as gorgeous version of Warner Stevens, standing before her.

She whirled to face him with those beautiful, yet startled blue eyes he always remembered, and loved looking into. Sure enough, it was Trinity Evans. His breath caught, and he smiled.

"What are you doing here?" he asked.

She seemed to deflate, and relax somewhat more. "I'm a reporter for the Chicago Tribune. They sent me of all people to do a story on....you know."

He gazed at her. "Following in your father's footsteps huh?"

Michael Evans, her father was a news anchor, very well known and highly respected in the area. His position also made things interesting when his middle son....the brother of a rookie cop at that....turned up missing from a three star hotel, with a 17 year old. Her brother was 19. People talked. It was a reason, once Trinity went to college, she *stayed* away. At least Warner felt pretty certain that was why.

"I'm just a reporter. I write. Nothing like what dad does."

Warner nodded. "Yeah, I remember you wrote for the school paper. You used to tell everyone you'd be a huge writer one day."

She smiled. Damn, she still had that same smile that used to drive him wild. He had always liked her, but was too shy to do much more about it than make idle conversation passing by in the hall, during or after school. Then, one Friday she asked him to go to a concert with her, Holly, and her brother Ben. Mrs. Evans had insisted they stay at a hotel overnight, to avoid being on the road too much.

He visibly swallowed a lump that had formed in his throat. If only they had just went against her wishes. Perhaps all four of them would have returned home.

"So….What's the deal with this story you have to do? To see if anyone can offer up any information of what became of them?"

Trinity shot him a look so intense, his heart skipped a beat. "If you must know, I'm doing this to get closure….My brother and best friend are dead. They have to be!"

A pair of eyes watched Warner and Trinity from across the street, following them as they eventually entered the hotel.

What the hell was she doing back here? It had been ten years. What could be bringing her back after so long?

The figure behind the eyes dialed a number on a cell phone. The other end rang three times before it was picked up.

"Hello?"

"She's back. What do you want to do about it?"

"You're sure you want to do this?"

"Do what?"

"Stay here. In this hotel,"

Trinity let out a breath she wasn't aware she'd been holding. No. She didn't want to do this. She had to. If it hadn't been for two of the other reporters on staff, getting bored one day and googling the names of everyone on the staff….none of this would have come about.

No one there had known about her past, why she even came to Chicago. Imagine the shock, discovering quiet, shy, and sweet Trinity Evans was involved in an unsolved disappearance case from ten years ago. Her brother and best friend turning up missing from a hotel, without checking out.

So, of course her editor jumped on the idea for a story. There was concern about whether she could do it or not. Trinity had to have a little time to think about it as well. It only took her over the weekend to decide.

"In order for me to write this story….the way it should be written….yes, I think I need to stay in this hotel…"

Warner had memories come flooding back to him as well, upon stepping into the Macfield Hotel lobby. He could remember the media frenzy in the lobby that day, once they realized Ben and Holly were nowhere to be found. He could remember being interviewed by the very news crew Trinity's father anchored for. Her oldest brother, Cole had been first on the scene, just starting out as a rookie cop at the time. Trinity didn't know who else to call. She had been so frantic, and upset.

Of course they had all been tested for drugs and alcohol, which they swore up and down they'd had none of. They were asked if either Holly or Ben had been under the influence. Had either of them been alone together or apart at any time?

The questions had been really grueling for both of them. The sad part was, they were all out just to have fun, and never really paid much attention. They couldn't answer a single question.

"I'd like a room too." Warner surprised himself and Trinity once they had reached the front desk. She had already paid for her room, with her credit card. She actually had requested the very room she had stayed in with Holly ten years ago.

"Warner…what are you doing?"

He turned to her, taking out his wallet. "I'm on vacation this week. To be honest, this ten year anniversary has been plaguing my mind too….and I've been thinking about you." he went on. "Considering we went through this together then, do you really think its fair for me to not be there now?"

She just continued staring at him in a look of total disbelief, which slowly turned into a look of admiration.

"Ok. As long as you room with me this time."

"She's staying there. In the actual room. Can you believe that?"

The voice on the other end of the phone laughed. "What does she think she's going to find there?"

"Hell if I know. He's there with her too."

"Warner?"

"Yep. I just called and found out they are both there."

"Ok…So, what do we do?"

There was a long, deliberate pause.

"Just wait….Until I give you the word."

Trinity and Warner reached the room, hand in hand. Trinity unlocked the door, and shaking, opened the door. The room looked exactly the same. She had more memories flood back of her and Holly jumping on the bed together, giggling. She slowly walked over to the bed, letting go of Warner's hand.

"Do you remember much?" Warner asked.

She nodded. "Yeah. We jumped up and down on this bed. We were so hyper after that concert…I don't even remember falling asleep," she continued, turning to face him. "In fact, the only thing I remember is waking up to find her gone,"

Warner stepped up closer to her. "Yeah…I think you came over, pounding on our door, and-that's when I woke up to see Ben was gone."

Trinity nodded. "Yes. I figured maybe the two of them snuck away for breakfast, or to the pool in back. But they hadn't. They never checked out, no one ever claimed to have seen them."

It became silent then. Trinity closed her eyes. "They have to be dead Warner. What other explanation is there for them to be gone without a trace, a word to anyone for ten years? Ben was a goof but never to that extreme, and I *know* Holly would have never done something so drastic."

Warner didn't say anything. Trinity went over to the only window in the room, which overlooked the street. He wanted to walk over behind her so badly, and hold her in his arms.

"It seems so stupid doesn't it? I can remember us being real hyper that night, but I can't remember going to sleep or even hearing Holly leave the room."

Warner sighed. "You know what I remember. Watching an X-rated movie with your brother. After that, my mind's a blank."

She shook her head, turning to him. "That's exactly what I mean! The way we are describing our memories…the only explanation could be that we were drugged or drunk, and all those tests came back negative. That only leaves one other option…amnesia."

Warner looked at her doubtfully. "Amnesia? Come on Trinity. I know you're wanting answers, but isn't that a little far-fetched?"

She looked at him with raw hurt in her eyes, that made him immediately regret what he said. "Trinity, I'm sorry. I understand how you must feel and believe me, I was there too, I know. You're suggesting we somehow had some sort of memory loss for a span of six to eight hours,"

Trinity gazed back at him now, with fear in her round, beautiful blue eyes. "That's why I'm here. We have to remember."

Just wait.

The voice released a frustrating breath, after hanging up.

Wait for what? There was nothing to wait for. She'd never figure out what happened. Every shred of evidence would never be found.

As for Warner….there was still some uncertainty with him. And perhaps that was why there was need to wait.

No matter what, the wait was going to be nerve wracking, not to mention hold the person's future in the balance.

Suddenly, Warner wished they could talk about something else….anything else but this. "You can't get out of doing this story? At all?"

She looked at him, exasperated. "Warner…Haven't you listened to me at all? I *need* to do this. To-"

"To get closure. Yes, I know. But….do you honestly think just writing a story on it is really going to do that? It's not going to help you understand what happened."

Trinity stood there, with her arms folded and her eyes narrowed. "Why are you back here? Why did you just happen to come by the hotel?"

"I told you….it's bothered me."

"Then why are you all of a sudden wanting me to forget it?"

Warner took his hands through his dark hair.

"You remember something don't you? Something you think is going to upset me."

"No, I don't. I….just want to talk about something else."

"Bull. You remember something. I can see it in your eyes. Tell me. When did you remember it?"

"Dammit Trinity, I don't remember! Ok? Can we…..just get out of here? Let's grab some coffee or something."

After a few long moments, she finally relented, thinking maybe he was right. "Yeah, that sounds fine. I'm really sorry Warner….This is driving me a bit nuts,"

He just nodded in understanding. "It's understandable….Come on, let's go. I'll treat you to some café mocha."

There was a Starbucks in town, just a few blocks from the hotel Trinity had no idea was now there.

"Yeah, we just got one about a year or so ago. In fact, my company is the one who helped construct it."

She raised her eyebrows. "Really? You're in construction?"

He nodded, sitting back in his chair, a proud smile decorating his face. "It was originally my uncles', then he fell ill, and couldn't manage it any more. He passed away about six years ago, so now it's fully mine, considering he had no children,"

She smiled, taking a sip of her coffee. "Speaking of children….Ever have any?"

He held up a finger. "One. A boy. He's three." he went on, already knowing what her next question would be, and stopping Trinity before she could ask it. "And no. I was never married to the mother. We dated for three months, before she ended up pregnant. She's married now, and we share custody of Sam." he went on. "What about you? Any guy been lucky enough to snag you?"

She quickly looked down. "No. Can't say they have."

She kept her eyes down on the table before her, feeling Warner's gaze.

"Geez…there must be a ton of idiots in Chicago."

She laughed. "You know, I almost forgot why I was so attracted to you in the first place."

His penetrating green eyes locked with her blue eyes, as the two shared a deep, intimate gaze.

"If….I had stayed here…..do you think it would have been us sharing a son together?" Trinity asked, not even believing she was actually doing it. She could tell it even surprised Warner. "Oh gosh, I'm sorry. I shouldn't have asked that, it was totally out of line!"

He started chuckling. "Trinity it's perfectly fine. Don't worry about it," he continued. "And to answer your question…it's hard now, to know exactly what the future would have held at that point in time. But I can honestly say it's something I would not have objected to."

It was growing dusk, when Warner suggested they go to Heyworth Park for a short stroll. The park had been a trademark hangout for them growing up. Despite the nagging in the back of her head to go back to the hotel and get to work on trying to write the story and sort through her buried memories, she went with him. She wanted to hold on to this time with Warner as long as possible.

She walked with Warner towards the playground near the entrance, reminiscing out loud. "Holly and I used to come here every day after school. We'd play Truth or Dare, and she'd come up with some crazy dares. I think once I had to flash every van that went by for five minutes!" She laughed.

Warner eyed her with a mischievous smile. "Where was I that day?"

She turned to him, her eyes sparkling. "I don't know. The main thing I remember that day, is the fact I was reported to the police, and Cole about killed me. He just promised me he'd keep a lid on it to our parents, after I threatened him I'd run and tell them I caught him making out with Holly."

Warner narrowed his eyes intently upon hearing that. "What did you say?"

She furrowed her eyebrows. "We had a slumber party one night, and dad was on assignment down in Florida, covering Hurricane damage. Mom was out of town too, on a shopping trip. Ben had brought in alcohol, and Cole stopped by…I was going into the bathroom, and there they were…Cole and Holly making out like crazy, he was standing at the bathroom counter and Holly had her legs around him, sitting on top of it, her butt in the sink."

Warner just stared at her, oddly. "I….thought Holly had it bad for Ben….not Cole."

Trinity stood there, what she was now remembering starting to make her shudder inside. "Yeah…she did. She liked Ben the moment she laid eyes on him, when we were in third grade. The crush followed her clear up to high school, I know because she drove me nuts with it."

They stood there in silence for the longest time, chills filling Trinity's spine as the implications of what a random memory, away from that night at the hotel was doing to her thought process. The chilling silence didn't end until Warner finally spoke.

"It's getting darker…I think we need to get back now."

A car sat at a discreet distance from Warner's SUV, the driver behind the wheel, watching as their two figures made their way back to it from the opposite direction. The driver shook their head, watching as the shadows grew closer in the ever growing darkness.

Where were they going now? It was growing darker and later. Maybe….just maybe….the two would get so caught up in old times, they would forget about digging into the past.

But….the driver knew they couldn't trust things to fall that way. They had to stay close to Trinity and Warner, as close as they could without being seen…..until it was time to face them.

Warner pulled into the parking lot of the hotel fifteen minutes later, after a horrendously silent drive. He shut the car off, and the two remained sitting there not moving or speaking. Finally after what seemed like endless minutes passed, she finally spoke, breaking the uncomfortable silence.

"Warner…..You don't think possibly…."

He turned to face her, his mind doing somersaults in debate as to whether to finally tell her the truth, what he could remember. He closed his eyes, tightly wincing. What would she think of him? After all this time?

"Warner?"

He opened his eyes, and looked into hers'. No, he couldn't do this. Who did he think he was kidding? He should have just let the past be, hell he had a son now! He couldn't afford to let anything get out. He shouldn't have let his hormones do…..

"Trinity…what are you doing?" he asked her as she took a hand down the length of his face. She had also grown much closer to him, so close he could smell the sweet scent of whatever perfume she wore.

"I don't know. All I know is, I don't like what is going through my mind and you're here and I really don't want to go back up to that hotel room….I just want to be with you. I don't want to think any more."

Before he could stop it, her lips were on his and his arms reflexively went around her body, as his lips returned the passionate kiss being delivered to them. He felt himself falling into a hot abyss, then he suddenly jerked up.

"What about your story?" he asked her.

She gazed at him, in the dimly lit car from the parking lot light above them. "It's not really my story anymore." This was her only response as the two fell into the seat together making intense love to each other, the passion from years past, exploding.

The driver had followed them back to the parking lot, and after waiting for what seemed like forever, they finally got up and silently went over to the car. The figure now was crouched down at the side of the car, their ear plastered to the door. Sounds came from inside, sounds that could only mean one thing. They smiled, getting out a cell phone dialing.

"What's going on?"

"They are sitting in the parking lot, making up for lost time apparently."

"What?"

"They're having sex, idiot!" The person hissed.

"You're kidding."

"No. I can hear them. I'm right outside the car."

"They can't see you?"

"No. I'm wearing all black."

"That's not going to guard against them spotting you! Warner isn't stupid, and neither is my sister."

The figure rolled their eyes. "Just trust me ok? I've gotten this far haven't I?"

There was a brief moment of silence, before the person on the other line replied.

"We can't afford to hold this off any longer. I need to face her and get this over with..." the voice went on. "Stay right where you are. I am on my way."

Trinity threw her head back in ecstasy as she climaxed, then cried out when her head hit the window.

"You all right?" Warner asked, out of breath.

She nodded, actually laughing as she grabbed the back of her head. Her blonde hair had come undone where she had it neatly styled in a barrette in the back. He couldn't help but laugh a little himself.

"Damn….I feel like I'm 18 again."

She giggled. "Yeah….It feels good huh?"

He smiled at her, touching her face where she had touched his just minutes ago. "It feels amazing, Trinity. God, I wish you had never left…." he went on, biting his lip. God, he had to do this now, after what they had just done. "….then maybe, I would have been able to tell you what really happened that night."

Her breath caught. She couldn't have just heard him right. "Excuse me? Did you just say you would have been able to tell me what really happened that night? After all the time we have spent together tonight, talking about how we couldn't remem-"

He held up a hand, stopping her. "Yes Trinity….God I beg for you to please forgive me and just listen. There is a very good reason why….I couldn't tell you. I was hoping you would just eventually forget it, we could go out, have some fun, catch up…."

"And do me in the front seat of your Blazer…..ooooooohohhhh…Go to hell, Warner! People told me you were a damned pig!"

She tried to pry open the door, only to have her arm grabbed by him. "Dammit Trinity, I know you are upset but you have GOT to listen, ok?"

"No, I don't!" she huffed in response, getting out of his hold and finally getting the door opened...to get out and run straight into her brother.

Cole smiled upon seeing her, grabbing hold of her. "Hey there sis. It's been a while. You should really visit more often."

She jerked away from him more in shock than anything else. She tried to smooth out the skirt she had been wearing, and shakily tried to fix her hair. "Cole, what are you doing out here? Outside Warner's car?"

He just shrugged. "This is my jurisdiction. My beat."

The other door shut, and Warner came around to them. "Cole, just leave her alone. We're not doing anything wrong."

"Besides messing around in the parking lot? I could get you both for public indecency."

"The windows are tinted. And….how the hell did you know what we were doing?" Warner asked, a hint of suspicion and fear seeping into his voice.

That was when the figure came around the side of the car, removing the black hood from their head as their face was revealed.

"Because I called and told him. I've been keeping an eye on you Trinity, ever since you stepped foot back here."

Holly smiled back at them, with different colored hair and some weight loss. Not that she had ever really been fat, but she had put on a little extra weight she had never been able to get rid of. And she never felt the need to. Besides, everyone thought she was gone, probably dead too. Which had suited her just fine. She didn't look like the same brunette everyone liked in high school.

"Geez Trin….you haven't changed much at all. No wonder Warner felt so compelled to still do you."

Trinity stood there, gaping at her, then all three of them. "What the hell is going on? Where's Ben? What is this? A sick prank that went ten years too long?"

"No, sis there is no prank. But I really wish you had not decided to come back here….At least not to hash all this stuff up. Everyone is happy, dad will be retiring in another few months. They are planning a trip together, they are even going to renew their vows. I am now in line for chief of police. Everyone is happy, happier than they have been in a long time." Cole said.

She shook her head. "Well…that's great and all but….I would still like to know what the hell is going on. I have a right to."

Holly rolled her eyes. "Oh for God's sake Trin!!! *I want to know what's going on, I have a right to!*" she mimicked in a high exaggerated voice. "Geesh, you were ALWAYS the party pooper! Never wanting to sneak a peek over at the men's locker room, never wanting to sneak in the back of the school to smoke weed….always the perfect girl…." she went on, coming up closer to her. "Why does everything have to be that way to you? Why can't you leave some stuff buried where it *belongs*?"

Before Trinity could respond to Holly's shocking temperament towards her, Warner stepped in. "Guys, stop it now. This is not going to accomplish anything," he went on. "I was going to tell her everything by the way, until you showed up," he said, looking at Cole with narrowed eyes.

Cole returned the glare, menacingly. "Why would you do that? Is whatever little thing you had for my sister years ago, and the romp you just had with her in the back seat of your SUV, really worth bringing all this up?"

Warner looked from him, to Holly then Trinity, who gazed back at him looking more vulnerable now than she did ten years ago when he found her, in tears and alone in the hotel room in the early morning hours. The same image that burned back into his mind upon entering the room just hours ago.

"Yeah," he said, slowly nodding. His gaze never fell from Trinity's eyes.

"Ok." Cole went on, aggravation apparent in his voice as he turned with a grim look on his face. "Let's go."

A half hour later, the four of them were in an area on the outskirts of town that Trinity was unfamiliar with. She was grasping onto Warner to keep from stumbling, in the dimly lit area although she wasn't exactly warming back up to him just yet.

"Where are we going?" she finally asked.

No one answered her until they reached an old dilapidated shelter. Her brother turned his flashlight up a beam, shining it around the makeshift shelter.

"Yep....This is definitely the spot. Haven't been here in so long I needed to double check." He turned to smile at the others. "Well sis....Do you remember anything yet?"

She looked at him, with confused disgust. "Why? Should I?"

Holly started to answer, but Cole stopped her and stepped over closer to his sister. "You and Holly started up a game of truth or dare that night....in the hotel. On a dare, you asked Holly to get Ben out of the hotel and *make out*," he went on, putting up his fingers in quotes. "What you didn't realize is, I was there that night too, with a room. Holly went to Ben's room first of course...in case you asked. Which was *her* mistake..."

Holly rolled her eyes visibly in the dim light from the flashlight illuminating the shelter area. "You are seriously never going to forgive me for that are you?"

"It's the reason we are even in this mess to start with, Holly!" he cried, turning on her angrily. "And...it's the reason Ben is dead today!"

Trinity was feeling lightheaded, as the confrontation wore on. It all became a blur in her mind, as she shook her head. She blinked suddenly, as reality and the present dawned on her.

She was no longer in the shelter but in a police interrogation room, sitting across from a heavy set officer, with piercing black eyes that studied her intently.

"Remember anything else?"

She stared at the metallic tabletop before her. "About that night ten years ago, or about what happened last night?"

"Either one."

She closed her eyes before speaking. "All I remember is daring Holly to go get my brother and sneak away with him to make out, away from the hotel. I knew she'd do it, she was the one nuts over him and wanting him along for the concert. I never wanted him along." she went on. "Also I knew if she left, that would give me some time alone with Warner. So a few minutes later I followed her over, to find Warner stepping out in the hall."

"And Warner told you she didn't leave with Ben?"

"Yes. And Ben had taken off himself. Warner didn't even know where he was. So naturally, I was worried."

"This prompted you two to go look for the two of them?"

She swallowed, her mouth growing dry. After requesting some water, she continued.

"We left the hotel, and that's when we saw Cole getting into his car and pulling away. We quickly tried to follow him, but he was going pretty fast."

"So….at this point, you had no idea he had been in the hotel?"

"No. At least I didn't," she went on. "We walked all around that night, and ended up at Heyworth Park. That's where I saw Cole's car parked. We heard arguing and, next thing I knew I could hear Holly screaming."

She gulped, as it all came rushing back to her like a horrid scene from a movie. It had been so dark that night, and she had been so scared and so confused. Warner had jumped in trying to break up whatever was going on, and she did as well. That's when the gun shot had rang out.

"You and Warner ran off after the gun went off?"

She could not control the tears that now ran from her eyes, dropping onto the hardened surface before her. "I don't know how I could forget something like that, for ten years just block it out! My brother was murdered, and…."

She trailed off and the officer finally finished the line for her. "And….thanks to you running again last night and calling us…we'll finally be able to solve this case,"

Warner had blocked the horrible memory out just like Trinity all those years, not remembering until being back up in the hotel….somewhat. He did remember more than her, and just chose to ignore it. That's what he admitted to the officer, breaking down. He had never heard what Holly said to Ben when he answered the door. He really didn't care, until he realized how much it affected Trinity.

Yes, he ran that night. He led Trinity right back up to the hotel. She had gone to her room and like an idiot he left her alone. When he did finally get worried enough about her, after trying to forget everything that had just happened….including the fact he had been wrestling Cole for the gun, to get it away from him. He had no way of knowing Cole was total sleaze, having sex with a minor…Holly….and jealous as hell of his little brother.

He also didn't know they had buried Ben behind that shelter where Trinity ran from after hearing the story. He had naturally ran after her, and hours later, here they now sat, being interrogated. Cole was basically going to end up losing his badge for helping to cover up a murder, and helping to give Holly Kingford an all new identity.

He didn't know what they were going to do to him or Trinity for that matter. And it scared him. He kept asking if he needed to get a lawyer and they didn't answer him.

He didn't get an answer for another two hours.

Trinity slowly packed what little she had come within the hotel room, a week later. She had been forced to stay an extra week to undergo court ordered psychiatric therapy, to decide if she had amnesia brought about by severe trauma, or if she did honestly remember possibly being involved in a murder all this time. After three long sessions with the doctor, a decision was made.

She was going back to Chicago. She not only had a story, she had a book. She planned to approach a publisher about it once back there. She would dedicate it in the memory of her brother Ben, who died for no good reason that night. To hell with trying to protect her family's reputation as Cole had put it.. Ben WAS her family

Since the gun was long gone which shot her brother....buried somewhere that Cole would not say...the police really had no way of telling who was responsible for pulling the trigger in the struggle that dark night. All they had was everyone's confessions. Cole's that he had followed them to the hotel that night not only planning to meet with Holly later and have sex with her, but under his mother's orders to have a cop keeping an eye on them. Holly's that, yes she had agreed to see Cole and was having sex with him since their freshman year...she had even gotten pregnant, and Cole had her secretly get an abortion! No wonder she had been a mess. Cole had really put on a good front for years, because he despised Ben. He was always Holly's first crush.

That night they had argued and Holly confessed to saying she wanted to end it with Cole. She had admitted all the time they were having sex, she was imagining him as his brother. This is what had led to Cole taking off with her. In fact, Holly said she thought he was going to kill her although he claimed he wasn't in the interrogation room. She thought this until Ben caught them leaving, wanting to know what the hell was going on. Cole told him to just come with them, there was no way he could allow him to just go back to the room now.

Trinity sighed heavily, sinking onto the bed. That was Bens' downfall. He always looked up to Cole, always did what he asked. He admired him for going into the public safety field. If he had just fought that night, made a scene, gotten someone's attention….everything could have been averted.

She couldn't think like that now. It really was the past, and it was time to let go no matter how sad and traumatic it had been.

She slung her bag over her shoulder, taking one last look into the room before telling it good bye. As she went down to the lobby, her eye caught the headline of that morning's paper.

"Three Jailed For Murder of Missing Boy."

She sadly thought about not only her family, but Warner. That was the worst part of this. He was only trying to protect her from the truth. He had remembered somewhat more, he just chose to ignore it. And now unfortunately she realized, a little too late she understood why. Now he was paying the price, just not as severe as the other two.

Then suddenly she knew what she had to do before she left. She had plenty of time before the flight.

Warner entered the room, with a frown on his face. The orange jail uniform clung to his thin but muscular frame. He had grown a beard in the short five day span he'd been in there.

"No word on how long they are keeping you?" she asked.

He sat down, crossing his arms. "Six months."

"Oh....Well, that's not so bad..."

"You tell that to the three year old boy who is wondering why his daddy isn't coming around." he went on. "Melissa won't even bring him here. In fact, she is now seeking full custody of them. She's afraid I'm some murderer she doesn't want Sam around."

Trinity's façade crumbled. "Oh, Warner.....My God I am so sorry. I wish now I had left things alone."

He gulped, his Adam's Apple bobbing up and down. "Trinity, as much as I want to blame you for this I am feeling real torn right now. I know you just wanted answers and I wanted to give you that much. I didn't know Cole and Holly were lurking around ready to pounce on us at any time. If anyone is to blame for this it might as well be me."

Tears ran down her face, blinding her eyes. "Don't blame yourself Warner. What you did was extraordinary. And....if you give me a chance, I will make sure your son knows that."

His gaze slowly fell, softly on her eyes. "What are you saying?"

"I'm saying, I'm going back to Chicago for now. I wrote the story last night in the hotel. And I'm going to look up publishers. I have a query for a book on it, I'm going to send around. Don't worry, it's going to be a fictional version, I am not using anyone's real names. But it is getting dedicated to Ben," she continued. "And in six months, when you get out, I will come back. If…you want me to. And I hope you do, because after that night in your SUV….I am finding it very hard to just let you go."

His gaze didn't waver as he looked back at her, a smile finally touching the corners of his lips. "I get out in four for good behavior."

She finally laughed, and smiled tearfully. "So, is that a yes?"

His gaze fell back on the table. "You sure you are willing to come back here?"

She nodded. "Yes. Besides, if I get this book deal I'll have to come back. Promotion…" she trailed off. "….And….I want to see who owns that shelter area out there where Ben is….I want to at least give him a memorial of some kind. He deserves that much."

Warner nodded in agreement. "Yes, he does."

She hesitated, sitting back. "There is one other thing bothering me…" she went on, in admission. "You somehow managed to remember more than I did, and you even acted different than I did that morning. I can remember actually feeling really odd. You just seemed quiet and troubled the next day through all the questioning."

Warner kept his head down for several moments then looked up and smiled at her. "Your brother had some sleep aids he brought. He never really wanted to come either that evening, and wanted to drug himself to sleep. They were pretty strong, he described them to me and they didn't show up in drug tests. When we came back that night, you were crying really loud. I knew you had to get some sleep, to prepare for the next day, and whatever we would have to face. So I brought some over to you."

Her mouth dropped open in shock. "So....you *did* drug me....it just did not show up."

He closed his eyes in a slight nod as an officer came in to warn them time was up. They each stood up, Warner smiling at her. Trinity had tears in her eyes, biting her lip to keep from breaking down. He then touched her cheek as she had done to his that night in the SUV.

"See you soon," he said before going back through the steel door to the jail cells.

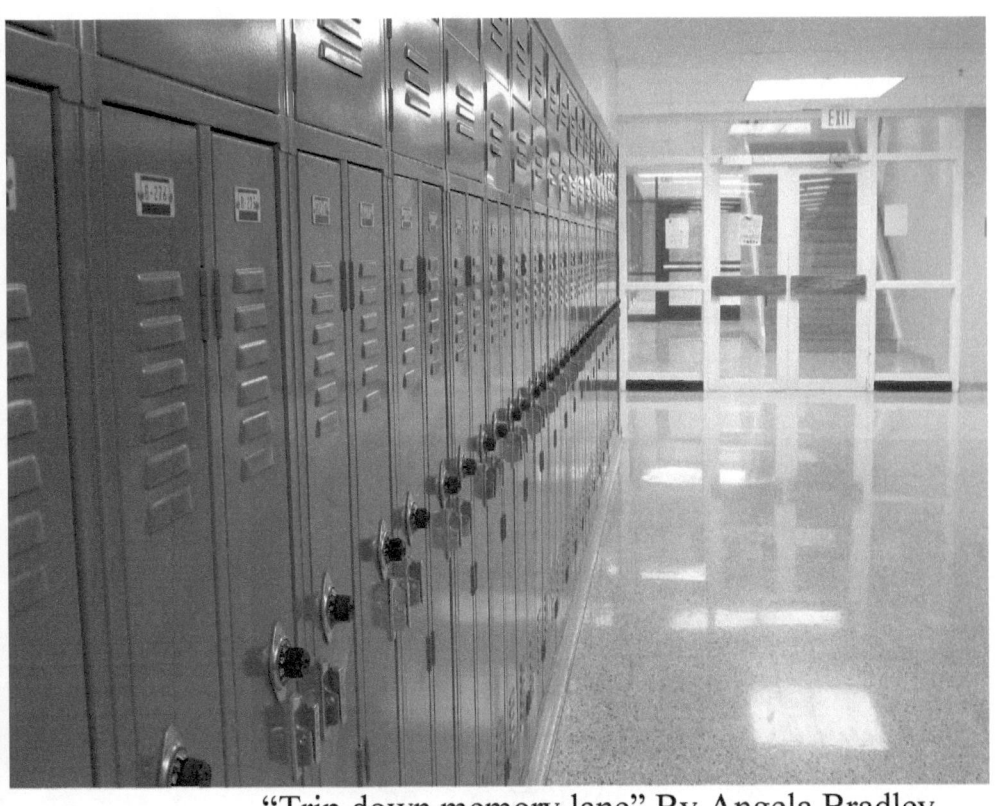

"Trip down memory lane" By Angela Bradley

A Year Gone so Quickly

Dark is the day,
We remember our friend.
Long gone, but still in our hearts.

A year has went by,
But no one has forgotten,
For his name is mentioned still.

He will wait for us all,
On the other side of this mortal realm,
And greet us at the gates.

He is a part of us all,
Everyone touched by him in some way,
And will stay with us forever.

As time goes on,
And days go by,
His memory is with us always.

But if for some reason,
I could someday forget,
God, Please remind me.

In Memory of
Christopher W. Hall

~Angela Rae

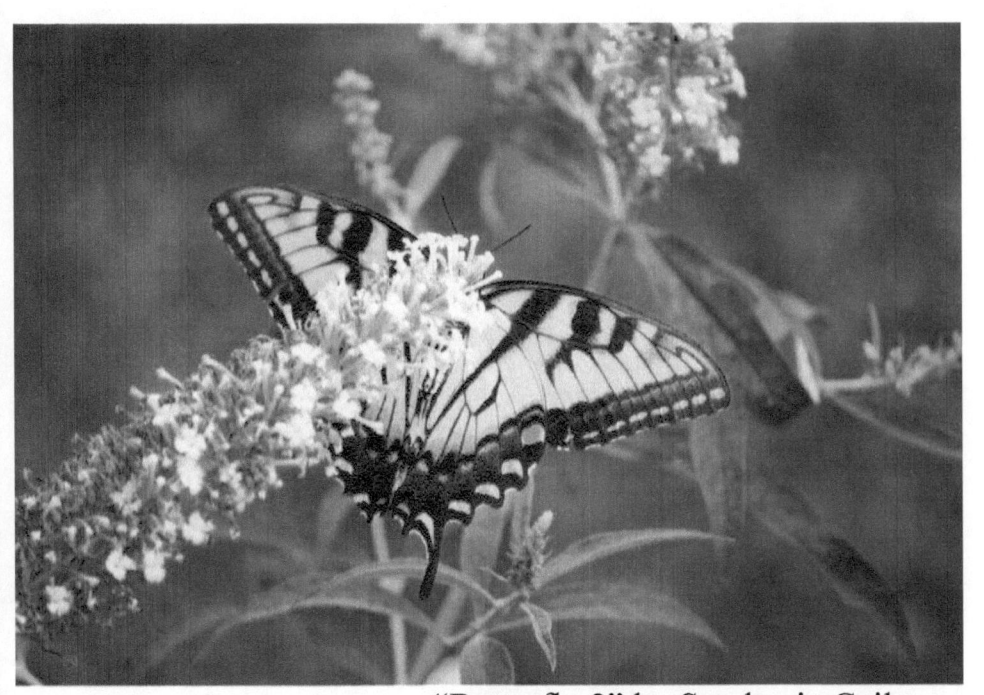

"Butterfly 2" by Stephanie Gailey

The Ones We Remember

Wish heaven had a phone
so I could hear your voice again.
I thought of you today,
but that is nothing new.
I thought about you yesterday,
and days before that too.
I think of you in silence,
I often speak your name.
All I have are memories
and a picture in a frame.
Your memory is a keepsake,
from which I'll never part.
God has you in his arms.
I have you in my heart .

~Glenn Huff

Wedding Day Wishes
To have danced just once with you
around the open floor.
To have heard you whisper an
encouraging word.
To have seen you smile and hold back tears,
while you laughed and wished us many happy years.
Though you were not here in body
my sorrow will lessen,
For you had a front row seat
watching me from heaven.

In memory of my Pappap.

~Angela Rae

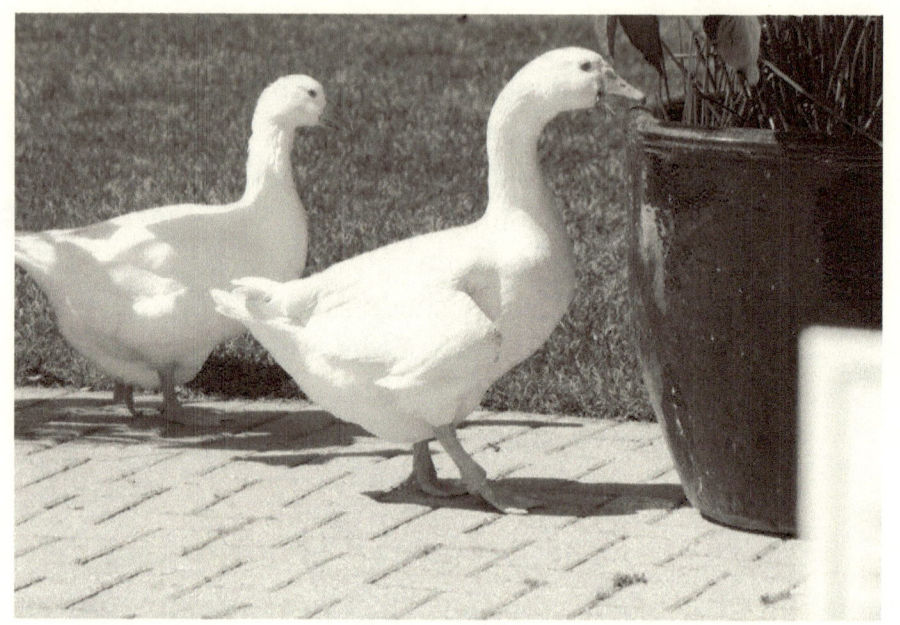

"Geese" by Stephanie Adkins

Crystal like are your bright blue eyes,
full of expressions that make me smile.

Chubby are your two little feet,
when I walk in the door you run to greet.

Your strong grip with those tiny hands,
God gave you, for which I'm sure he has plans.

Your smile makes me happy; your laugh makes me cry,
with joy in my heart, I wipe the tear from my eye.

I can't imagine my life where you were not in it,
you've grown so fast, I only blinked for a minute.

Your first birthday soon will be here,
and Mommy's voice will be the loudest to cheer.

In honor of my son, Caden.

~Angela Bradley

The following is a short story by Anonymous

Agape Love   **Anonymous**

They are like a well oiled machine. As they age they become more of one than the original couple. Where one is starting to weaken, the other is still able. Together they work out their plan. It keeps things normal. There is a total ritual that dad performs each morning when he rises. He moves quietly because she still sleeps after tossing and turning all night, listening to talk radio in her earphones. He waits patiently for her to arise; slowly walking down the hallway emerging into the Family Room. He smiles like he smiled the first time he met her. His love for her transcends all time. He says, "Give me a kiss." She robotically retorts, "NO!" He laughs at their little joke. She will always be his little doll, sitting on the edge of the pool one hot Summer day. What a comfortable love they have. Agape love, indeed. He's 86, she's 85. Forever and always.

To be so blessed. It is hard to find in today's society. But, what a blessing it has been for me, all my life to watch their trials and tribulations shouldered together, as one unit. Hard to do. Hard to find. Hard to maintain. But they never gave up. Never even thought about throwing in the towel. Agape love.

So here we are at the cross-roads of life where Parent becomes Child and Child becomes Parent. Where did the time go? Why are our bodies failing us? In our hearts we are not here - at this age in time. We are lost somewhere in the past when we were star struck with love. And now, when he calls me "MeMe, Jr." and I call him "PapPap." We have to laugh. You remember it, those days when everything your parents did got on your nerves. When did the switcheroo happen? How is it that now everything they do becomes precious with repetition? The calm of their structured plan; she needs that to feel at ease. He understands because they function as one and so it works. Can we?

So, when she wants to watch Dr. Oz like the housewives of the 50's watched the afternoon soaps, he lets her because her mind is still working, thinking all the time, hardly ever at rest. She forces the stimulation on herself because she is afraid if she doesn't she may not be able to hold this thing at bay.

So, every day I say to God, "Thank you for Dr. Oz because he is obviously a caring individual who is sharing medical information with the lay person in their own terms." She is fascinated. She is intrigued. She should have been a nurse because she has always been such a lovingly stern care giver. Stern that she made you do what you were "supposed" to do and lovingly because you knew she was motivated by her love for you. Hard combination to pull off, but it's always been there.

But on some days I would like to personally get my hands around Dr. Oz's neck and squeeze until he said, "UNCLE!" But of course, I don't. Like today for instance, he talked about aneurisms. I'll be danged if she doesn't think that *I* have all the symptoms and if I don't stop doing so much and running around so much and not getting enough rest so much, WELL, I might just find that one day my head will explode from a brain aneurism.

Thank GOD my husband has a good sense of humor. If not, that might just get on your nerves a little bit. But he calls her, "My favorite mother-in-law," and she calls him "My favorite son-in-law." He deserves the title. He is so kind to them. He is patient with them. He does for them without their asking. He really loves them. I'm so blessed.

So today we found out my husband does NOT need another back surgery. We celebrated with a nice breakfast at Eat n' Park. That's his favorite meal to eat out - breakfast. Now we are referred to a back rehabilitation doctor. The next step in the process but we are both relieved he does not need surgery. So, we have to form a plan. Do what we can when we can and when we are able. Work through it together. Because that's what God wants us to do, together as one.

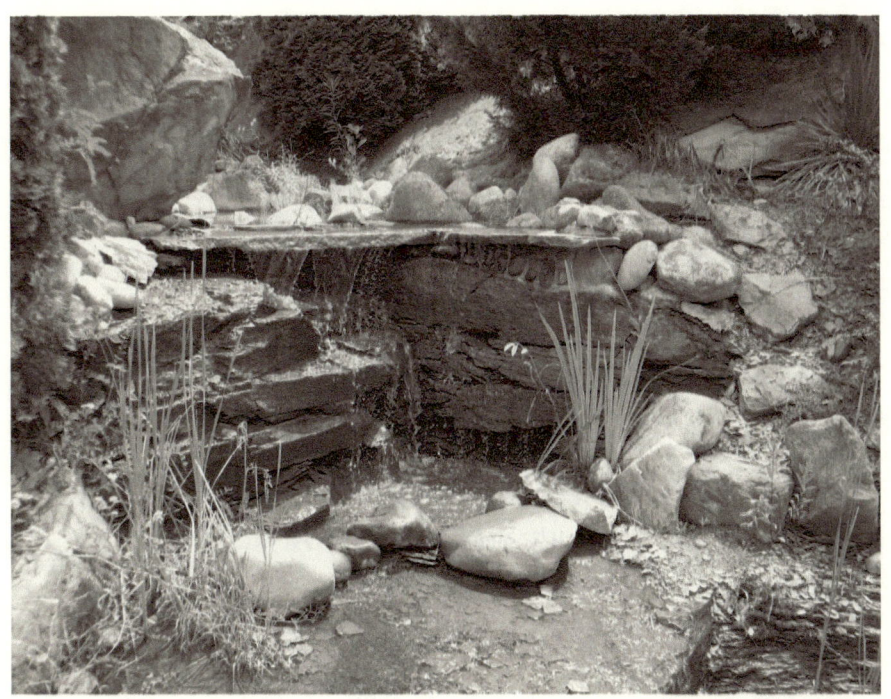

By Angela Bradley

One Voice Amongst a Crowd

I speak, but no one hears me.
I shout, but no one knows.
I scream at the top of my lungs,
That's just the way it goes.

We all must speak together,
Individuality is not allowed.
Cause no one would ever listen,
To one voice amongst a crowd.

~Angela Rae

Man of My Dreams

We've traveled cities,
and braved the fiercest night.
You've sometimes had to choose,
and your choice is always right.

My Knight in shining armor,
a man that sweeps my off my feet.
You're always the winner,
there's no one you couldn't beat.

Yet I notice,
you're not here with me.
We're from different worlds,
it's not really meant to be.

The books are endless,
I could read all night long.
You're tall and handsome,
or you're brave and strong.

Cause you are as they write you,
you're not really real, you see.
But when I read, at times,
you sure seem real to me.
~Angela Rae

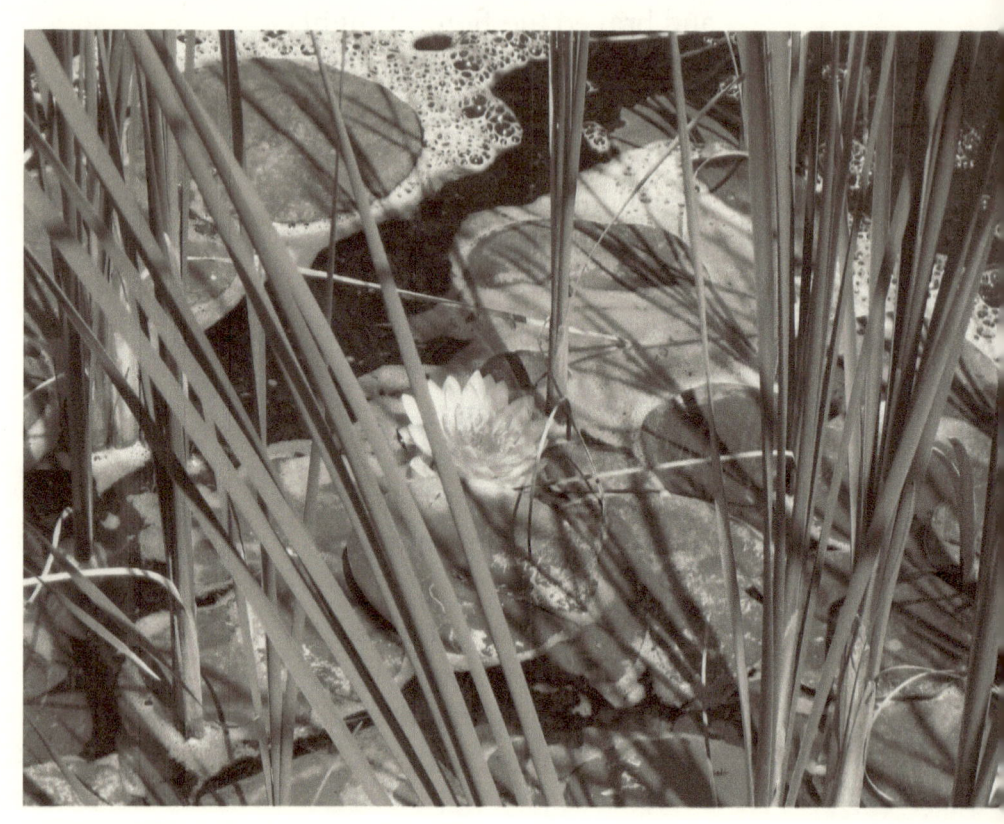

By Angela Bradley

A world,
Of witches with cauldrons bubbling,
And warlocks with staffs of power,
And dragons with silver tips on their wings,
And princesses with names of a flower.
Where kings rule over kingdoms,
And magic flows through the air.
All I do is close my eyes,
And find myself standing there.

~Angela Rae

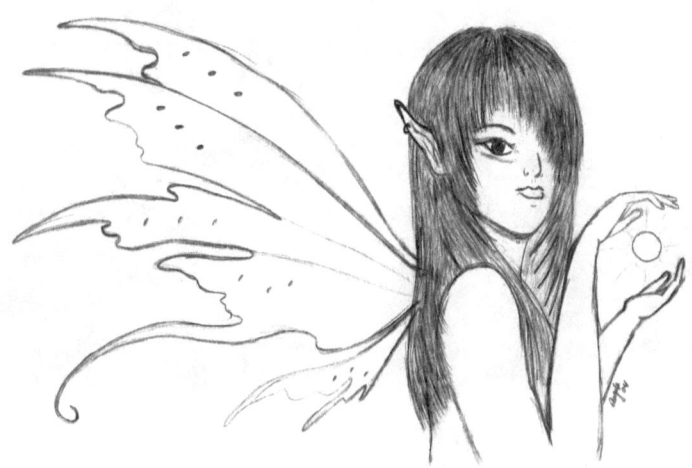

By Angela Bradley

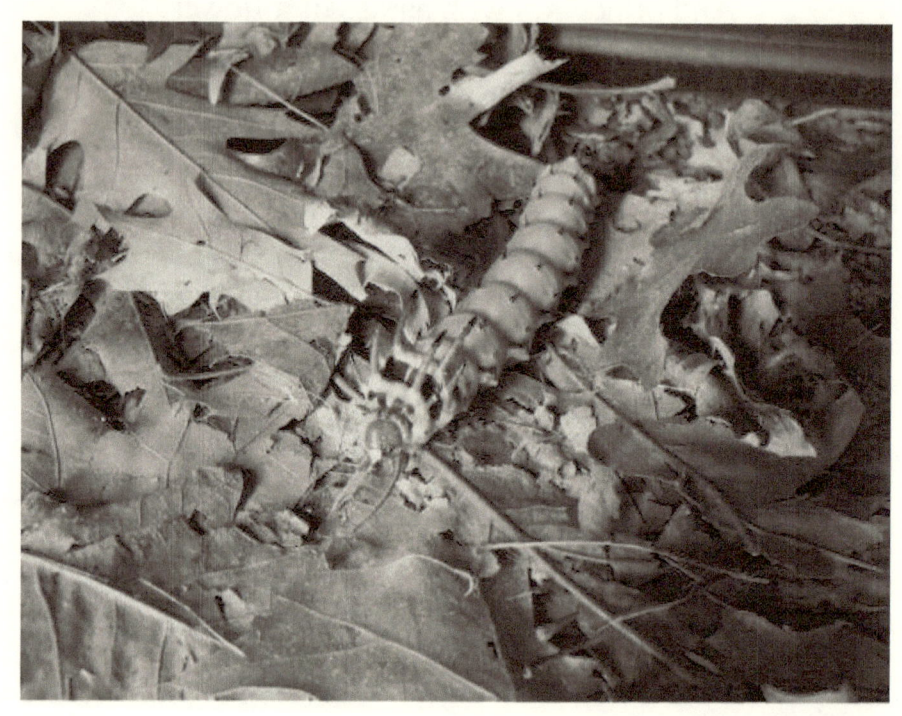

"HUGE Caterpillar" by Stephanie Gailey

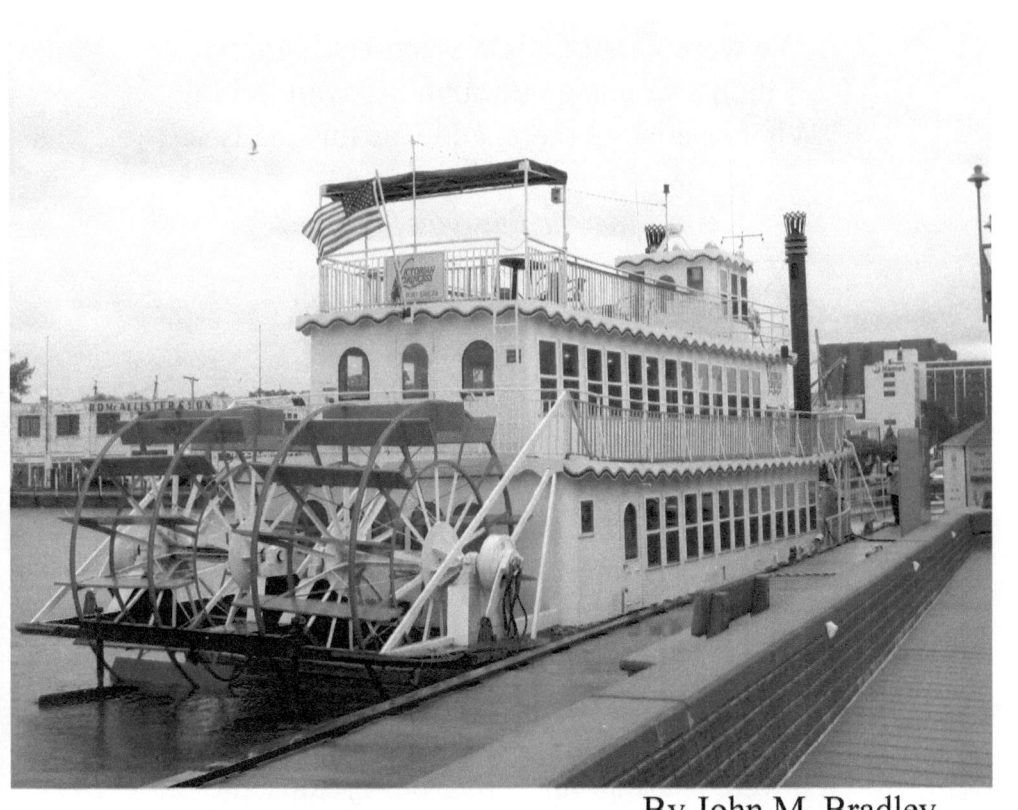

By John M. Bradley

Am I?
Lyrics written by Angela Bradley (2004)

When I broke it off the first time around,
We were young, this was a great big town.
I didn't wanna go through life wonderin',
What else is out there, and was this really it?

Am I the Air that you breathe?
Am I the Words that you speak?
When you reach out at night,
Am I the one that you seek?

Am I the girl of your dreams?
Am I the love of your life?
And someday soon,
Will you be calling me "Wife"?

Graduation Day was approaching fast,
We were talking and laughing, we were having a
blast.
We were sharing our hopes, our dreams and our
plans,
And what do you know, we were soon holding hands.

Am I the Air that you breathe?
Am I the Words that you speak?
When you reach out at night,
Am I the one that you seek?

Am I the girl of your dreams?
Am I the love of your life?
And someday soon,
Will you be calling me "Wife"?

Our love was tested…
And you almost failed…
But we talked through it, we sorted things out,
And we've been together damn near 3 years now.

(Instrumental)

Relationships are hard, but with one good as ours,
Lovin' comes easy when it's straight from the heart.
I think of you, and hope you're thinking of me,
When I think of my future, you're all that I see.

Am I the Air that you breathe?
Am I the Words that you speak?
When you reach out at night,
Am I the one that you seek?

Am I the girl of your dreams?
Am I the love of your life?
And someday soon,
Will you be calling me "Wife"?

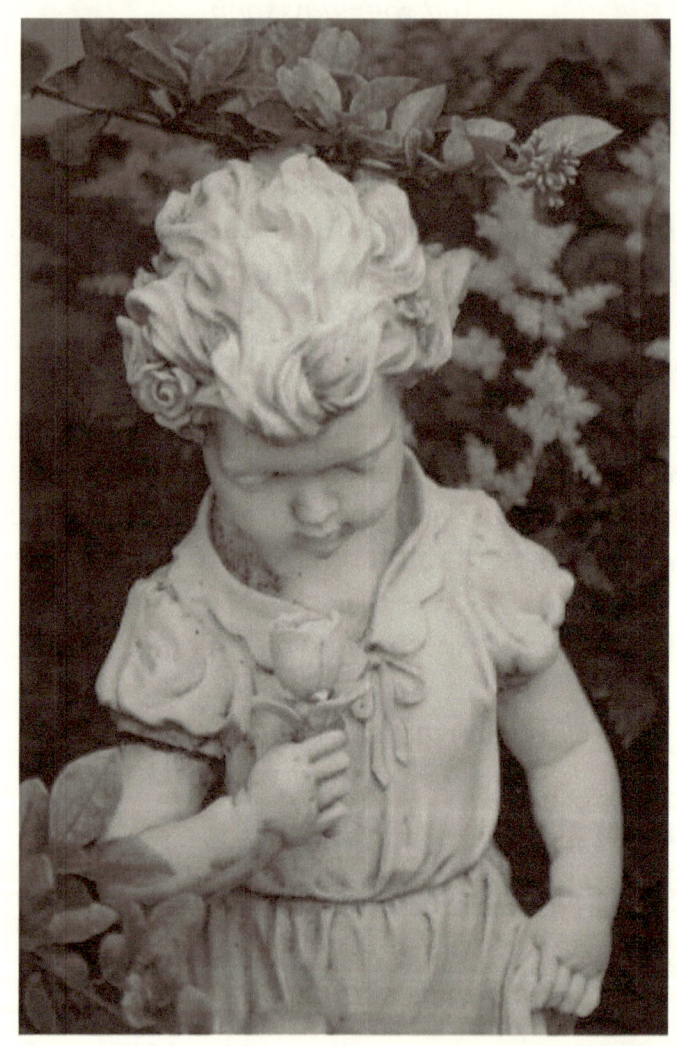

"Statue" by Stephanie Gailey

I'm not allowed to hate you.
But you hurt me so much.
I didn't realize the que.
Was your chilled touch.

How can I believe again?
After you still drew the knife.
Is loathing you a sin?
Who's to know if I'll survive this life.

I walk alone with these open sores.
still dripping with scarlet tears.
You hollowed out my very core.
I wander in wide-eyed fear.

-Angela Robyn

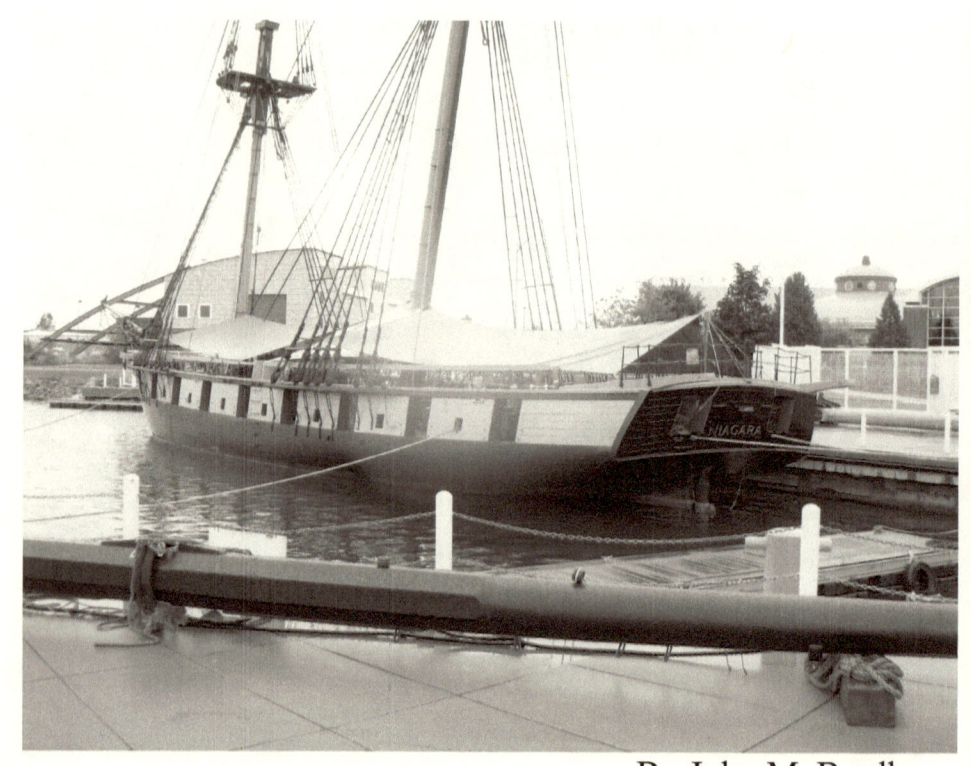

By John M. Bradley

The danger deepens.
you can tell by it's laugh.
this wicked banshee.
It tears me in half.

I must hurry.
To protect this light.
'Screech', I hear it.
Urgent to get out of sight.

Halting to a stop.
I stand my ground.
To this ungodly essence.
Unwillingly I have found.

To prove my clarity.
I simply set the light free.
My demons are gone.
All along, I've held the key.
-Angela Robyn

Silent Sentinels

The white stone crosses sit
like silent sentinels marking
the way.
Waiting for the soldiers
to come ashore like they did
on that dreary June Day.

Some of the young soldiers
were scared! But with what
courage they had saved,
they stormed the Normandy
beaches wave after wave.

Some were lucky and made it
all the way up the shore.
Some never made it past
the landing crafts ramp door.

Although the machine-guns
fire was deadly they charged
on just the same.
Each and every soldier claimed
a place in fame.

The years have gone by and
these young men have grown

older and some have passed away.
The old soldiers still
here can remember that fateful day.
Some go and visit the beaches
where brother soldiers fell.
Still in their minds they
hear a wounded soldiers yell.

They walk along the shoreline
and see the tree limbs sway.
Then they visit the stone
white sentinels, that still mark the way.

-John Sherbine

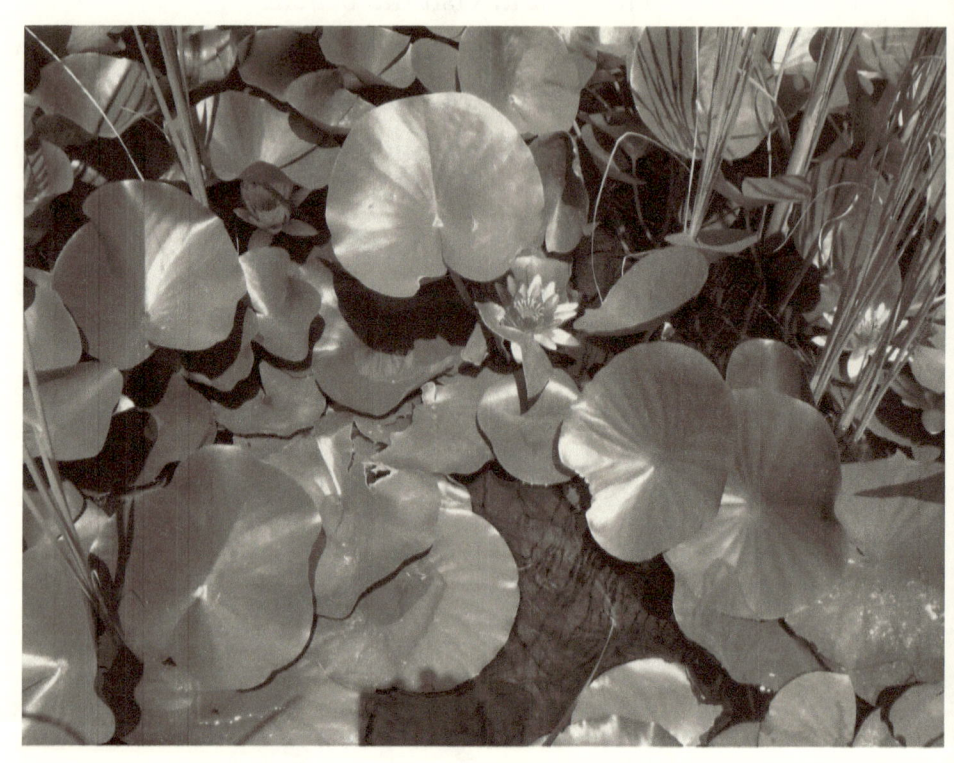

By Angela Bradley

It's now been a year
since you've left us here
and went to walk with the Lord.

I keep watching and waiting
and anticipating
for you to come up the basement door.

I listen for the yell
of mom giving you hell
for doing something you shouldn't have done.

And I wish nothing more
than for you to adore
and be Pappap to my son.

It all feels so strange
this gradual change
that we are all trying to get through.

It's been pretty rough
we're trying to be tough
but our family is missing you.

In Memory of my Father.
Raymond J. Ristau
Aug 29 1958 – Oct 30 2010

~Angela Bradley

The following is a short story by Angela Rae

The sky was a beautiful blue as I drove through Green Township heading down Eaton Road towards home. I felt like today was a day, just like any other, little did I know things would take a tragic turn for the worse.

I came up to the intersection at Millers Hill and proceeded to go, when someone's tires screeched as they peeled out of Exxon, then slamming into me, hitting the drivers' side door.

Everything flashed in my mind, flooding my head with memories: my childhood, my first days of school, my first kiss, my family, friends, and my fiancé.

All I could see was white at first. Then I felt the sensation of separation, followed by a feeling like I was floating.

I looked down and saw myself. Blood trickled down the left side of my forehead and from my nose. The entire drivers' side was smashed in. I watched as a crowd started to gather. Police and an ambulance came to the scene, but I heard no siren.

The man that had driven the car that hit me was sitting on the curb while an EMT assisted him. EMT's and police wrestled my car door open and pulled my limp body out. They laid me on a gurney and a woman checked my pulse. She shook her head sadly.

I began screaming "What are you people doing? Help me!"

No one looked at me, no one could hear me.

They covered me with a white sheet and loaded me into the ambulance. I wanted to cry, "No! Stop! Here I am! Don't leave me here! I'm too young! I'm too young!"

I drifted back down to the ground and looked at the guy who had hit me. He was a young boy, younger than I, and he was crying. I couldn't hear anything, but I could read his lips. He kept saying over and over, "I'm so sorry, I'm so sorry!"

Anger overwhelmed me. I hated this boy so much. He ruined my life. I clenched my fists, not sure what to do with myself at that moment, just knowing that his words could not undo what he had just done.

Then I felt a sudden rush of forgiveness as I looked at his grief stricken face. As the boy was loaded into a second ambulance, I closed my eyes and said aloud, "I forgive you."

When I opened my eyes, all I could see was a thick white smoke, billowing from the floor. I looked around and saw….. nothing. Every way I turned was endless nothing.

I turned back around and a middle-aged man stood before me dressed in black.

"Hello Nadine," he spoke calmly, "I'm Gabriel."

For a moment I could not speak. I could only stare, confusion surely showing all over my face. I finally found my voice and asked the first question running through my mind.

"Am I in Heaven?" I quietly asked.

He smiled at me, "No my dear, this is the entrance to Purgatory." He waved his hand and a grey door appeared out of nowhere.

"Wow" I looked at him in awe.

"Before you enter," he stepped closer to me, "Nadine, I'm going to give you a choice." His tone turned very serious, "A choice that few people sent to Purgatory

get. If you wish, you can accept your fate and spend the rest of eternity with the millions of other people not good enough for Heaven, yet not evil enough for Hell." He paused briefly, watching my face for a reaction, "Or you can choose to make a difference in people's lives."
I thought a moment about what he just said; trying to decipher what he was telling me. "What, exactly, do you mean?"

"You could become an angel." He smiled.

"But I thought people in Heaven were angels?"

"Not quite, my dear," he put his arm around my shoulders "You see we recruit people from Purgatory to become angels so that the Heaven sent are able to…relax. Most of them have had hard enough lives, we want them to enjoy eternity." He finished explaining.

"What would I be doing as an angel?" I enquired.

"You would be sent on routine jobs, meet lots of people, help talk people into or out of stuff, as the situation calls for, that sort of thing."

"Like a guardian angel?" He nodded at my question. Things were clicking in my head now. "And people could see me?"

At this he shook his head. "Only those you are sent to help can see you, no one else other than your own kind." He added quickly "No, you could not visit your loved ones."

"But I'd be sent back to Earth, I could see them?" a little hope came back to me when he nodded. I stared at the door for a few minutes, seriously giving this some thought.

When I turned back to him, he smiled as though he had already known my decision.

"I want to be an angel!" I said with enthusiasm.

"Good!" he clapped his hands and a soft glow seemed to surround me. I felt a warmth spread through my body. I closed my eyes and let it consume me. When I opened them again, I felt a sense of happiness.

"What, no wings?" I joked. Do angels joke? I thought.

He waved his hand, gesturing at myself, "They are there, you just don't need them yet."

"But how will I…" he cut me off.

"When the time comes, you'll just know. There is much about this job that is strictly intuition," he stood a little straighter, "Now go, there are other angels down there who will help you along the way. You'll know who they are when you meet them." He nodded his goodbye, and disappeared.

I would like to thank everyone who

helped make this book possible.

Glenn Huff - Poems

Stephanie Gailey - Photos

John M. Bradley - Photos

Angela Robyn - Poems

John Sherbine - Poems

Jennifer Brown – Short Story

Pastor Jim Parkinson - Poem

Alice Proudfits' Family – Poem

Your donations helped make this book a success.

If you would like to donate to the next composite book,

please email for more information at:

myfundraisingefforts@yahoo.com

www.ingramcontent.com/pod-product-compliance
Lightning Source LLC
Chambersburg PA
CBHW022123170526
45157CB00004B/1737

* 9 781105 383359 *